EDGE BOOKS™

HORRIBLE THINGS

Terrifying, Bone-Chilling Rituals and Sacrifices

by Kelly Regan Barnhill

Consultant:
David D. Gilmore
Professor of Anthropology
Stony Brook University
Stony Brook, New York

Capstone press®

Mankato, Minnesota

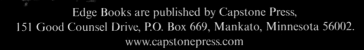

Edge Books are published by Capstone Press,
151 Good Counsel Drive, P.O. Box 669, Mankato, Minnesota 56002.
www.capstonepress.com

Library of Congress Cataloging-in-Publication Data
Barnhill, Kelly Regan.
    Terrifying, bone-chilling rituals and sacrifices / by Kelly Regan Barnhill.
    p. cm. — (Edge books. Horrible things)
    Includes bibliographical references and index.
    Summary: "Describes a variety of rituals practiced by different cultures
in the past" — Provided by publisher.
    ISBN-13: 978-1-4296-2295-0 (hardcover)
    ISBN-10: 1-4296-2295-4 (hardcover)
    1. Rites and ceremonies — Juvenile literature. 2. Human sacrifice —
Juvenile literature. I. Title.
GN473.B37 2009
306.4 — dc22   2008028865

Editorial Credits

Aaron Sautter, editor; Ted Williams, designer; Jo Miller, photo researcher

Photo Credits

Alamy/Danita Delimont, 26; Gianni Muratore, 23; Ian Dagnall, 29;
    vincy lopez, 24; Winston Fraser, 9
AP Images/Malcolm Browne, 13
Art Resource, N.Y./Erich Lessing, 18
Chris Mathews, 10
Getty Images Inc./Gaye Gerard, 17; Hulton Archive, 15; Hulton Archive/
    George Pickow, 6; The Image Bank/Grant Faint, 4; Marilyn Angel
    Wynn/Nativestock.com, 11; Patrick Landmann, 8; Robert Harding
    World Imagery/Sylvain Grandadam, 22; Stone/Terge Rakke, 27;
    Time Life Pictures/Mansell, 16
The Image Works/HIP/Print Collector/Pierre Fritel (creator), 20
Mary Evans Picture Library, 12; Stacy Collection, cover
Newscom/AFP Photo/Mark Ralston, 14

1 2 3 4 5 6 14 13 12 11 10 09

Table of Contents

WITHDRAWN

Do You Feel Courageous?

The native warriors gather in the flickering firelight. The air smells of smoke and sweat. Drums throb while the warriors pray, sing, and dance. They believe their rituals will bring good fortune in the coming battle.

Rituals are words and actions that define people's beliefs. Every **culture** has its own rituals. In the United States, people watch fireworks on the 4th of July to celebrate their freedom. At Greek weddings, people break dishes for good luck. During the Chinese New Year, people perform the Dragon Dance to scare away evil spirits.

Many rituals involve singing, dancing, and eating lots of food. But other rituals can be dangerous or even deadly. People have been disfigured, endured horrible pain, and even died as a result. Are you ready to learn about terrifying rituals and sacrifices? Turn the page to see if you'd have the courage to perform any of them!

culture — the way of life, beliefs, and traditions of a group of people

Mummy Makers

More than 100 mummies were found near Mexico City in the early 1900s.

For thousands of years, people have wondered what happens after death. Every society has its own beliefs about life after death. In ancient times, many people believed the dead needed their bodies for the afterlife. For this reason, they preserved dead bodies as mummies.

Long ago, turning dead bodies into mummies was a common practice. Mummies have been found all over the world. In the Middle East, people used wax to preserve bodies. In Peru, the cold, dry climate created mummies naturally. In ancient Israel, people treated bodies with oils and spices. Then they wrapped the bodies in cloth.

HORRIBLE FACT

Sometimes mummies are made by accident. The climate surrounding dead bodies can preserve them. Bodies can dry out quickly in a desert or at the top of a mountain. Some mummies are found in peat bogs. The peat keeps the bodies from rotting away.

The ancient Egyptians used a complicated process to make mummies. First, priests took out the body's organs. They placed the organs in clay jars. The heart was considered the most important organ. It got its own jar. However, the brain was considered completely useless. The priests simply threw it out. Then they laid the body in a dry chamber and covered it with salts and spices. Finally, they tightly wrapped the body in strips of cloth and placed it in a **sarcophagus**. Thousands of years later, we can see these mummies in museums around the world.

sarcophagus — a stone coffin

HUNTING TROPHIES

The preservation of dead bodies is still practiced today. Many hunters like to keep their biggest kills as trophies. The animals are preserved with a process called taxidermy. Skilled taxidermists can preserve the animals in certain poses. For example, a bear might appear to be growling or attacking.

Self Mummification

2

Self-mummified monks can still be seen in Japanese temples.

It's one thing to mummify someone else's dead body. But can you imagine becoming a mummy while you're still alive? Hundreds of years ago, Buddhist monks performed a self-mummification ritual in Japan. For three years, the men ate only seeds and nuts. They also exercised often. When they were very thin, the monks stopped eating completely. They drank only a kind of tea made from the sap of the *urushi* tree. The tea helped to preserve the monks' organs after they died.

When a monk felt his body was ready, he sealed himself in a tiny tomb. He had only an air tube and a bell. Every day, he rang the bell to show he was still alive. When it stopped ringing, everyone knew he had died. The monks were then considered almost as holy as a god.

FASTING AND VISION QUESTS

Many religions around the world practice fasting, or ritual starvation. People usually fast to have a strong spiritual experience.

Some American Indians use fasting to discover their path in life. During a vision quest, young people fast and pray while they wander through the wilderness. They often stay awake as long as possible too. They keep wandering until they have a vision about their future. When they return, they're no longer thought of as children. Instead, they are considered adults with a clear purpose in life.

3

Self Immolation

Long ago, women in India often jumped into funeral fires to be with their dead husbands.

Setting oneself on fire is called self immolation. Why would people willingly burn themselves to death? It's an extreme way for people to express their devotion and beliefs.

In India, women once practiced *sati*. When a man died, his body was burned on a large wood pile. The man's widow would then throw herself into the flames and was burned to death. It was a symbol of her devotion to her husband. *Sati* is illegal in India today, but it was practiced for hundreds of years.

An Extreme Sacrifice

On June 11, 1963, a Buddhist monk named Thich Quang Duc set himself on fire in South Vietnam. Through it all, he simply sat and calmly prayed. He did this to protest the abuse of Buddhists in his country. The picture of his burning body soon appeared in newspapers all over the world. Because of his sacrifice, many people learned about the crimes of the South Vietnamese government. By November, South Vietnam's leaders were removed and a new government was created.

HORRIBLE FACT

According to legend, Duc's body was reduced to ashes, but his heart didn't burn. Duc's heart was placed in a Buddhist temple as a holy object.

4

Chinese Foot Binding

Foot binding is illegal today. But a few women still went through the ritual in the early 1900s.

Hundreds of years ago, young Chinese girls often went through a painful ritual. When a girl was 6 years old, her mother began binding her feet. First, the four smaller toes on each foot were broken and bent beneath the foot. Then her feet were wrapped in tight bandages. As she got older, the bindings got tighter. The goal was to keep her feet from growing more than 6 inches (15 centimeters) long. Eventually, her feet became permanently hook-shaped. She would be in constant pain for the rest of her life.

How Chinese foot binding started is a mystery. However, small feet were once a symbol of beauty and status in China. Most men thought tiny feet were very attractive. They wouldn't marry a woman if she had large feet. Many mothers didn't want their daughters to work for a living. They put their daughters through the painful ritual so they could marry into a wealthy family.

TINY WAISTS

While Chinese women suffered from bound feet, women in Europe suffered too. Europeans prized tiny waists as a symbol of beauty. To achieve this, tight corsets were tied around girls' waists. Every year, the corset was pulled tighter and tighter. Corsets were so tight that women had trouble breathing and often fainted. The corsets caused serious injuries too. Many women suffered from broken ribs and spinal problems.

5 Gladiators

The Romans watched and cheered as the gladiators brutally fought to the death.

The year is 100 AD. In the city of Rome, Italy, two deadly fighters face each other in an arena. They are perfect warriors with dangerous weapons and lots of training. A huge crowd cheers as the fight begins. One man will win. The other will die.

HORRIBLE FACT

Gladiators were usually slaves. Winners often earned money to eventually buy their freedom.

The gladiator games were an important part of Roman society. Romans prized courage in battle. But what does a warlike society do when there are no wars to fight? For the Romans, it meant watching warriors try to kill each other. The games were a form of entertainment. Thousands of people filled arenas to watch the gladiators fight to the death.

TODAY'S VIOLENT ENTERTAINMENT

The gladiator games seem gruesome to us today. Why did people cheer as someone was slaughtered with a sword? Yet similar violence is still shown in today's movies and TV shows. Many horror movies show people being killed in brutal ways. Thousands of people enjoy watching professional wrestlers beat each other up. People aren't killed for our entertainment any more. But these shows may help us understand why the gladiators were so popular in Rome.

6

Human Sacrifices

The Maya often sacrificed people on special altars (front) near large pyramids (rear).

Hundreds of years ago, the Mayan Empire ruled much of Central America. The Maya had an advanced **civilization**. They had several large cities and a complex written language.

At first glance, the Maya might have appeared to be peaceful people. But their culture also had a dark side. The Maya often sacrificed people to their gods. Mayan priests usually sacrificed a young boy no older than 12.

First, the victim's hands and feet were tied. He was then laid on an altar and held down. The crowd hushed as the priest slid his knife into the boy's chest. Then they cheered when he pulled out the boy's still-beating heart! The Maya believed these sacrifices pleased the gods.

civilization — an organized society

HORRIBLE FACT

The Maya practiced human sacrifice to receive different blessings from their gods. Sometimes they wanted the gods to bring them good fortune in battle. Other times they wanted a good harvest for their crops.

Many other cultures in Central and South America practiced human sacrifice. Perhaps the most violent were the Aztecs. They believed their sun god was easily angered. They worried that he might stop the sun if he became angry. The Aztecs performed constant sacrifices to keep the sun god happy. It's believed the Aztecs sacrificed at least 20,000 people every year. They also practiced **cannibalism**. After sacrificing a victim, they offered the heart to their gods. Then the priests would cook and eat the rest of the body!

cannibalism — the practice of eating the flesh of another person

ACCUSING THE ENEMY

Sometimes, groups of people have been falsely accused of performing human sacrifices. Why? Their enemies made up the stories so they had an excuse to attack. During the Middle Ages, some people falsely accused Jewish priests of killing and eating babies. This was a horrible lie. But it sparked hateful attacks on Jewish people that lasted for many years.

HORRIBLE FACT

Incan priests often sacrificed children to their gods. First, they drugged their victims so they couldn't escape. Then they took the children to the top of a mountain. They believed the gods lived there. Finally, they choked the children to death and left their bodies on the mountain.

Polynesian Tattoos

Native Polynesians still go through a long, painful ritual to get their tattoos.

In ancient Polynesia, tattoos showed a person's social standing, family history, and job. Children received their first tattoo at age 12. They received more tattoos as they grew older. Chiefs were often completely covered with tattoos.

HORRIBLE FACT

Polynesian women were limited to tattoos on their lips, ears, hands, or forearms.

MODERN TATTOOS

Today, tattoos are a popular form of body art. The process is basically the same as the Polynesian tattoo. But modern tattoo artists use clean equipment to avoid infections. Some people enjoy extreme tattoos. Their faces and bodies are completely covered in wild patterns and colors!

Getting tattooed was a slow, painful process. Tattoos were created with a sharp comb made of tortoise shell. The village priest first dipped the comb in ink. Then he placed it against a person's skin and began tapping it with a small hammer. The sharp comb pierced the skin to push in the ink. When the comb was pulled out, the ink was left behind. The priest then mopped up the tiny drops of blood that oozed out. Blood was sacred. It couldn't be allowed to fall to the ground.

Fire Walking

Walking on fire is an important spiritual ritual in several cultures.

In India, a pit of red-hot coals smolders at the edge of a village. The village priest and his followers march slowly toward it. They sing songs and pray. Soon, they take turns walking barefoot across the burning coals. They believe that if their hearts are pure, their flesh will not burn.

In parts of Africa, fire walking is used as a type of ritual healing. It's believed that evil spirits cause sicknesses. In order to heal someone, a healer fasts and prays. Then he walks across hot coals to purify himself. Finally, he lays his hands on the sick person to drive away the evil spirits that cause the sickness.

HORRIBLE FACT

Trained fire walkers rarely suffer serious injuries. They walk quickly and confidently to keep their feet from being burned.

ONE HOT MOVEMENT

Sometimes, people practice fire walking for personal reasons. In the 1970s, Tolly Burkan began teaching people how to walk on fire. He believed that if people could walk on hot coals, they could accomplish anything. Today, more than 3 million people have followed his example. They believe walking on fire gave them much more confidence. They now enjoy challenging themselves to do things they were too scared to do before.

Land Diving

Land diving is a thrilling ritual for the young men who perform it.

On Pentecost Island in the Pacific Ocean, several young men breathe hard with fear and excitement. In front of them stands a high wooden tower. They are about to leap from youth to full manhood.

The ritual they're about to perform is called *Naghol*, which means "land diving." During the ritual, the young men climb to the top of tall towers and tie vines to their feet. Then they gather their courage and leap off. They trust that the vines will keep them from hitting the ground. It's believed this ritual first began as a way to ensure a good harvest. It later became a symbol of a boy's change into manhood.

HORRIBLE FACT

In the 1980s, people in North America became interested in land diving. The practice inspired them to create a new extreme sport — bungee jumping!

DIVING DANGER

In 1974, England's Queen Elizabeth II traveled to Pentecost Island. She wanted to see land diving performed in person. Unfortunately, there was a terrible drought that year. The vines were dry and brittle instead of soft and springy. Many divers hit the ground when their vines snapped. One young man died from his injuries.

Explore it in Person

Where can people go to learn more about the customs and beliefs of different cultures? One of the most interesting places is the Smithsonian Institute's National Museum of Natural History in Washington, D.C. The museum contains millions of historical **artifacts**. From mummies to sacrificial altars, each exhibit gives people a glimpse into the past.

Learning about a society's hopes and fears helps us understand its rituals. We can then know why even the most bone-chilling rituals are still performed in some parts of the world.

artifact — an object made and used by people in the past

Millions of people visit the Smithsonian's Museum of Natural History every year.

Glossary

artifact (AR-tuh-fakt) — an object made and used by people in the past

cannibalism (KA-nuh-buhl-izm) — the practice of eating the flesh of another person

civilization (si-vuh-ly-ZAY-shun) — an organized and advanced society

corset (KOR-set) — a fitted undergarment used to give women a fashionable figure

culture (KUHL-chuhr) — the way of life, beliefs, and traditions of a group of people

protest (PROH-test) — to object to something strongly and publicly

sacrifice (SAK-ruh-fise) — to kill an animal or person to honor a god

sarcophagus (sar-KAH-fuh-guhs) — a stone coffin

society (suh-SYE-uh-tee) — a group of people who share the same laws and customs

Read More

Martin, Michael. *Inca Mummies: Sacrifices and Rituals.* Mummies. Mankato, Minn.: Capstone Press, 2005.

Masoff, Joy. *Oh, Yikes! History's Grossest, Wackiest Moments.* New York: Workman, 2006.

Ripley's, Inc. *Ripley's Believe It or Not! Special Edition 2009.* New York: Scholastic, 2008.

Internet Sites

FactHound offers a safe, fun way to find educator-approved Internet sites related to this book.

Here's what you do:

1. Visit *www.facthound.com*
2. Choose your grade level.
3. Begin your search.

This book's ID number is 9781429622950.

FactHound will fetch the best sites for you!

Index